T0198994

# UNSTUCK

One Heroine's Journey of Art and the
Courage to Live on Purpose

Vicki Todd

Balboa Press books may be ordered through booksellers or by contacting:

Balboa Press
A Division of Hay House
1663 Liberty Drive
Bloomington, IN 47403
www.balboapress.com
1 (877) 407-4847

ISBN: 978-1-5043-4763-1 (sc)
ISBN: 978-1-5043-4764-8(e)

Library of Congress Control Number: 2015921371

Print information available on the last page.

Balboa Press rev. date: 1/27/2016

BALBOA
PRESS
A DIVISION OF HAY HOUSE

Also by Vicki Todd:

Floater No More: How the Courage to Walk through an Open Door Changed Everything, a chapter in *20 Beautiful Women Volume 2: 20 More Stories that Will Heal Your Soul, Ignite Your Passion, and Inspire Your Divine Purpose*

This book is dedicated to all the Wild Woman Spirits who howl at the moon and dance to their own beat.

"Tell me, what is it you plan to do with your one wild and precious life?"

Mary Oliver

# Contents

# Foreword

There are numerous artists on the planet, each with a unique message to share and an original approach to sharing that message within their chosen medium. In addition, there are other creative individuals who are willing to be vulnerable by writing an autobiography as a way of sharing their message.

Vicki Todd has decided to jump all in and let her Wild Woman out by creating her unique approach to giving us her personal story - demonstrated through her art. Some of her paintings have their stories written out beneath the exquisite presentation while others leave you wishing for the written story as well so you can take it in through all the senses possible.

As a student, professor, and contributor in this field, Vicki Todd has brought her own exquisite, intelligent, gifted, and playful touch to each of her paintings, her creations, as she must since each represents an aspect of her personality.

As a psychotherapist in private practice for over 25 years and as a president of the National Speakers Association in Connecticut I have literally witnessed thousands tell their story yet Vicki Todd's delightful and creative way touches both the child and the adult in you simultaneously.

Participate in the transformation of a woman as she grows and progressively becomes more and more of who she was meant to be, one painting at a time.

As a student in this art form, ever growing and enhancing her skills she delights in walking this path with you; as a professor she is delighted to encourage you to do the same and as a contributor she wants you to thoroughly enjoy this multi-leveled journey through her life.

Anything is possible in the world of art and to see where this woman goes next will be a delight but first begin this journey of one woman who has taken her art to the world and out of her studio and her classroom reaching and delighting a far greater audience.

Dorothy A. Martin-Neville, PhD
Coach/Mentor, Author, Speaker, Consultant

# Preface

*Unstuck: One Heroine's Journey of Art and the Courage to Live on Purpose* is a visual memoir about art – more specifically my art and how it has impacted, colored and served as a gravitational pull throughout my life. It is also about the courage to make life-altering transitions to move closer toward my True Self and life's Purpose.

I once heard Deepak Chopra describe one's life Purpose as a mountain. He said a person's inner wisdom will guide her along the winding path around the mountain moving ever upward toward the peak, which is that individual's unique reason for being on this earth. The Purpose may be hidden from time to time like a path overgrown with brambles and weeds and require effort to discern and clear. At other times, the path toward Purpose is evident and smooth, easily traversed. The individual walking this path must be willing to listen to the cues her soul whispers to discover her Purpose and find the strength to reveal her self-in-potential.

I'm listening intently to my soul's whispers. I've discovered my mountain is art.

However, the path to this discovery has had many twists and turns. I've flipped my life twice - become unstuck from two life circumstances that were blocking my path toward evolving into my True Self. During the first flip, I morphed from a nonworking wife in a failing marriage who had just lost a baby I wasn't meant to conceive into an independent university professor. More recently, after discovering my life's Purpose through meditation, I resigned from my secure, 11-year tenured professor position to follow my bliss of art.

This blind leap of faith may seem crazy to some, but in my heart I knew my soul would slowly expire if I didn't follow the path toward truly honoring my Purpose. I would become a dead woman walking.

We all have a Calling – a Purpose - in life, the gifts that we were given at birth we're meant to use to serve the world. *Unstuck* tells the story of how I've realized and moved toward fulfilling my Purpose. My hope is that you will recognize yourself in my story. Your Purpose and life circumstances are unique to you. You may be able to easily weave your Purpose into your current life, making it more vibrant and textured, without causing cosmic shifts that rock your world. Or, maybe you – like myself – feel the need in the depths of your soul to take a more pronounced leap of faith into the unknown to fully spread your True Self wings. Either way, I hope that reading *Unstuck* will reverberate with you and inspire you to fulfill your own unique Calling, whatever form your mountain path takes.

Are you ready to listen to your soul's whispers and climb your mountain toward your True Self? The world is waiting for you to honor your Purpose and share your Gifts. Let's shine together!

# Introduction

Happy, Texas: 1971
A true one-act play featuring the inner dreams of a 6-year-old girl.

**Prologue:**

The location is a large wooden stage in the school auditorium of the rural 670-ish person town on a hot July evening. The town's people are mostly farmers, cattle ranchers and devoted housewives. There is only one school in town – home of the Happy Cowboys and Cowgirls – five churches, no stop light on the red brick main street. It's a close-knit community, in which everyone knows everyone (and everyone's business/ secrets).

The scene begins with the 6-year-old GIRL on the large stage. Her doting mother has entered her in the Little Miss Happy beauty pageant. She wears a pink frothy dress, white ruffle bobby socks, and black patent Mary Janes. Her hair is perfectly coiffed by her doting mother – blonde ringlets hang perfectly, just touching her slight shoulders. The GIRL stands alone on stage with the pageant's JUDGE, Kenneth Wyatt, a professional artist who paints western/cowboy-themed oil paintings. It's the Q & A portion of the pageant. The lights of the packed auditorium are dim except for the bright spotlight on GIRL and JUDGE.

JUDGE: (speaking into hand-held microphone) And, what's your name, little girl?

GIRL: (speaking into microphone offered by JUDGE, serious expression) My name is Vicki.

JUDGE: And, what would you like to be when you grow up, little girl?

GIRL: I want to be an artist.

Some people in the dark audience giggle aloud at the GIRL's response.

CURTAIN

**Epilogue:**

At the conclusion of the pageant, the GIRL is crowned Little Miss Happy. A sparkly crystal tiara is placed on her blonde head and a white sash with Little Miss Happy printed in gold glitter is placed around her shoulder and torso.

When the mother and GIRL are in the auditorium's foyer after the pageant's conclusion, a few town's women ask the mother if she had coached the GIRL to say, "I want to be an artist," hoping to win over the professional painter JUDGE. The mother is surprised and replies, "No – she said that all on her own." The GIRL keeps her artist desire safe – a seed waiting to bud and blossom at some unknown point in the future.

END

# Here's Where I Thought My Heroine's Journey Began

"If you could be anything in life, no fear, no obstacles, what would that be?"

This was the question Deepak Chopra asked during a meditation session I was listening to in the summer of 2013.

"An artist," was the answer that flashed into my mind like a Broadway marquee sign.

I immediately began weeping! How could this thing I loved so much throughout life - the thing that I had been surrounded by since helping my Grandmother in her china shop and oil painting classes as a child in little, rural Happy, Texas – be the purpose for my life? Art was supposed to be a part-time, fun hobby. Not the main focus of my existence…

Or was it?

The clues were scattered like breadcrumbs creating an obvious trail to this meditation moment. A photo of me as a 3-year-old toddler taken by my Grandmother in her art studio surrounded by oil paintings. The memory, retold countless times by my mother, of me answering "an artist" during the Little Miss Happy beauty contest at the age of 6 when the judge, southwest painter Kenneth Wyatt, asked what I wanted to be when I grew up. Encountering my first naked boy in my very first art class – a live model class - the summer after graduating from a sheltered upbringing in Happy High School. The handful of art classes I took in college as electives because my mom had urged me to major in something that would "make money." And returning to painting as a purging emotional release in 2001 after divorce, going back to school for a doctorate degree, and preparing to move from Texas to Connecticut alone to begin a new life as a university professor.

Vicki in her Grandmother's art studio

Examining these clues, art was present during pivotal moments in my life. I finally realized that I should actually thank my ex-husband. If it weren't for him and the turmoil caused by the abrupt life shift from nonworking wife, who had just lost a baby I was not meant to conceive, to professor, I would have never painted Inner Beauty Blooming, the first of my series of visual diary portraits and the birth of my art ambitions that bubbled to the surface while meditating in 2013.

I wasn't sure at the time exactly how my art equaled my Purpose. All I knew for sure was that I could use my art in some way to inspire others. Then I heard Elizabeth Gilbert talking about Joseph Campbell's The Hero's Journey on Super Soul Sunday while promoting her book, *The Signature of All Things*. She described how she had encountered her Call to Adventure that prompted her to leave her traditional married existence and travel to three countries in one year, the creative kindling for *Eat, Pray, Love*. She described how Alma, the heroine of her new novel also walked this journey.

So, I researched the steps of The Hero's Journey, and discovered my initial Call to Adventure occurred much earlier.

# Here's Where My Heroine's Journey Actually Began

**The bathroom floor.**

I found myself kneeling there quietly praying and sobbing in 1998, my husband sleeping in our adjacent bedroom. That was the year of my Seven-Year Itch. I always joke that my Seven-Year Itch came in the form of my mother badgering me to have a child, just one, so I could have the close relationship she and I had always enjoyed.

The problem was I never wanted to be a mother. Even at the young age of 6, my mom said I defiantly told her that I didn't want to do what she did, become a mom and housewife. But here I was on the cornflower blue bathroom carpet that came with the house I had purchased seven years before, quietly crying and imploring God, "I don't want to be married. I don't want to have a baby. I feel hopelessly stuck. HELP!"

You see, I've always considered myself a floater in life never having a clear vision of what I wanted to do or be. That's why I got married. I graduated with a bachelor's and master's within five and a half years, and the next logical step seemed to be marriage. After all, that's what my mother, aunt and two grandmothers had done – found a mate and settled down. I later learned on an episode of Oprah that these are called shadow beliefs. We tend to follow the path of those who have gone before us, even if that path – at least in my case – feels a bit off.

I had even quit my communications job to help my husband manage the hair salon he wanted to open. Another shadow belief right on track: none of the females in my family had worked outside the home. The husbands had always been the sole breadwinners. By my Seven-Year Itch, I had been a nonworking wife for four-plus years. My world reduced to answering the phone at the salon, painting a ton of ceramics while waiting for the phone to ring, taking violin lessons, playing violin in the church orchestra, and adopting a "grandmother" at a nearby nursing home. Add to that caving into my mother's pressure to have a baby, enduring the nightmare of fertility medication, not feeling joyful upon becoming pregnant, being admonished by my mom about not being joyful, finally getting on board with the motherhood idea, and then – BOOM – losing the baby in the 11th week.

During all of this turmoil that had become my life because of the choices I'd made trying to fit into society's "norm," my identity and self-esteem were cowering face down in the corner. That's why I was sobbing on the bathroom floor during the night asking God for a new direction.

The Universe answered with an open door of opportunity that changed the trajectory of my life.

In July of 1998, my former dean at Texas Tech University had seen the feature story I'd placed in the newspaper promoting the salon. He recognized that I wasn't working in a formal job, and called to ask if I would teach a summer writing class that started the NEXT day – only two short months after my miscarriage and the thud of my self-confidence hitting rock bottom!

I was shaky, but I said yes to this open door of opportunity. I knew my marriage was failing and teaching was a key to independence and freedom. So, I accepted this Call to Adventure, which led to getting divorced, earning my doctorate degree, and moving from Texas to Connecticut solo in 2003 to begin a new existence as a university professor – a 180-degree shift from my previous self.

For some reason, I had the idea that returning to painting, which I hadn't done since college, would be a welcome outlet from my apprehension during this tumultuous period. I found it to be an emotional release, a way to purge my feelings of anxiety, fear, hope, anticipation, and determination. My art began taking shape in the form of female portraits surrounded by emotion and femininity. I eventually realized I was painting a visual diary of what was happening in my life, a visual memoir. The female faces may have come from free-hand sketches of women in perfume ads and fashion photos, but the themes and emotion driving the works were from my life experiences at certain snapshots in time.

Following are the three portraits I painted before moving from Texas to Connecticut and beginning a new life.

Inner Beauty Blooming

# Inner Beauty Blooming

The initial thing that struck me about the photo my Grandmother took of me as a toddler in her art studio – a photo I discovered in a family photo album during Christmas 2013 – was that the first portrait I painted in 2001, Inner Beauty Blooming, has the same off-to-the-side stare looking toward the same direction and wary facial expression! When I painted Inner Beauty Blooming, I had no recollection this picture even existed.

The thought behind Inner Beauty Blooming came after my divorce and going back to school to earn a doctorate degree – insurance I could always take care of myself and survive after not having a job for four-plus years to manage the salon my soon-to-be-ex-husband and I had started together. I was not the moneymaker in the business, only the manager. When the opportunity popped up seemingly from the blue – Divine Order anyone? – to teach the summer writing course at Texas Tech University, I nervously jumped at the chance. Excellent student evaluations and encouragement from my dean prompted me to pursue a doctorate degree, eight years after completion of my master's, and begin the journey of self-preservation. Even though I was scared and angry to be in the position to have to start life over after marriage, I completed my doctorate degree and landed a job as an assistant professor at a private university in Connecticut – a huge leap for a girl who had lived her whole life in West Texas and left all friends and family in Texas to start totally over in the North East. A new adventure and life!

Hence the name and concept behind Inner Beauty Blooming. The facial expression serious, a little wary and looking toward a hopeful, although unknown, future.

Defiance

# Defiance

We've all felt defiant or acted defiantly at some point in our lives. Some of us on a daily – maybe hourly – basis. That's what this painting is about…acting defiantly.

Imagine that you know you will have to move because of a job. Imagine that to some extent you have a choice of where to move for that job. Imagine that the little voice inside of you says, "Go for it! Take a risk! Let's try something new!" So, you listen to that little voice inside and move 1,700 miles from Texas to Connecticut…alone…with no friends or family waiting to welcome you on the other side.

Now imagine how you would react if at first your family in West Texas wasn't quite so supportive of this leap. What if your parents – although they are very proud today – had the initial impression that you must not love them anymore if you wanted to escape to a "foreign" place so far from home. Even a cousin looked as though you'd punched him in the stomach to think that you'd even consider leaving the Lone Star State.

But what if that little voice inside is louder, more persistent, more certain than any of these outside voices? What if you knew you had to give this a shot and accept the adventure or you knew you'd regret it forever?

That's how I felt when I painted Defiance. I knew this was my chance at a new beginning, a fresh start. Even though I had huge doubts of the unknowable outcome, I had to do it for me no matter how it affected others. The girl's posture and facial expression are haughty – her eyes not quite in focus – seeing a future that's not quite formed. She defied the naysayers and carved out a niche she could call her own life – a defiant decision she does not regret.

Sea of Hope

# Sea of Hope

Sea of Hope is the last portrait I painted before leaving Texas. It's the flip side of Defiance. For all the bravado and grit that make up Defiance, Sea of Hope portrays the girl who grew up in a traditional Leave It to Beaver household and is scared, feeling rudderless. No female in her family had ever done what she was doing, so there was no pattern or role model to emulate. She's a pioneer exploring her own individual frontier.

I had seen a black and white photograph of the poet Edna St. Vincent Millay in a magazine wearing her old-fashioned dress standing beneath the branches of a magnolia tree. For some reason, this image intrigued me, so I turned it into this painting. The girl is the old me following the life pattern I had observed of graduating college, getting married, living a traditional existence. But that little experiment just didn't work for this girl. So, she's chosen a new life far from home to start over, apprehensive, excited, petrified, yet eager. She's tentatively clinging to the branches of the tree – so hoping that her new uncharted life will be alive, vibrant and fiery – like the blossoms on the tree. The flowers are pointing upward symbolizing her fervent hope that this new life will be beyond all she can dream - her Sea of Hope.

But without me telling people what the paintings meant – the hidden messages behind a certain expression, use of color, reason for a flower - the viewer would not be able to discern that a message existed.

So, I took a shot at explaining the meanings and the life story progression of my first three portraits to a guy I'd met in a singles Sunday school class with whom I'd gone on a few dates after my divorce. Huge mistake! As soon as the words left my mouth, I immediately wished I could stuff them back down my throat! I felt so exposed, naked, vulnerable!

I swore I would never again share my paintings or their very personal meanings with anyone unless they were close friends or family. Just the thought of letting the outside public view my artwork gave me a case of nerves and dread.

After this vulnerable experience, my painting came to a halt as life marched forward. I became consumed with navigating a new town in a new state and trying to decipher the ins and outs of a tenure-track assistant professor position at a new university. The heavy cardboard box of acrylic paints I'd drug from Texas to Connecticut sat in the floor of my closet gathering dust. I only painted two additional portraits after making my big move. My art had become a forgotten part-time hobby pushed to the back burner.

Fast-forward a decade to summer 2013 when my life's Purpose emerged during Deepak's meditation. With that simple answer of "an artist" bursting into my consciousness, I soon began to feel a second life transformation taking root.

My intuition started urging me to share my art and writing beyond the walls of my home and pages of personal journals. So, I put my fear of showing my work aside and created a website, vickiworldart.com, that contains photos of my portraits and blog stories about the life circumstance behind each piece. I believed my story of flipping my life from a stagnant position of nonworking wife totally dependent on her husband to an independent professor was an account that could inspire others who may feel stuck in their lives.

However, I soon began perceiving that showing my work on a website was not enough. The Universe was asking me to answer a more profound Call to Adventure that would take me closer toward my True Self and Purpose. I loved teaching my students, but I knew in my heart that becoming a university professor was not my ultimate calling in life.

Drowning Violet

# Same Song, Slightly Different Verse

I don't know about you, but some songs can create a deep emotional reaction in me. Even if you haven't heard the song in years, it can take you right back to that place like a time machine. All of a sudden you're that past person with the same feelings, remembering the sights and smells like you had never left that place.

In his book, *The Untethered Soul: The Journey Beyond Yourself*, Michael Singer, proves that I'm not totally crazy. Singer says that unfinished energy patterns from the past are called Samskara in the yogic tradition, and they are buried deep down as impressions we'd like to forget or avoid. However, Samskara from past experiences can be stimulated by new events, even if those current events aren't identical to the past experiences, causing us to relive thoughts, emotions and sensations that we underwent in the past. Singer claims that if the past experiences were painful, then the stimulation of the Samskara by current events will also be painful.

This is exactly what happened beginning in the spring 2014 semester when my university took a nosedive into chaos brought on by major financial issues. This was a very dark time, and the fallout included surprise firings of several tenure-track faculty members, cutting part-time faculty budgets, and omitting programs with low student enrollment numbers. A dark cloud of dread hung over the once-cheerful campus.

It was the same song with a slightly different verse. Just as listening to a song from my past can drag up memories and emotions that I thought were long forgotten, the chaos at my university stirred up the same feelings I'd experienced in 1998 when I lost the baby and my marriage began going south after I started teaching and decided to earn my doctorate degree. My feelings of being trapped, suffocated and wanting to escape a bad marriage and stagnant life circumstance seemed to equal my situation of feeling trapped and suffocated by a job I no longer found fulfilling that was denying me the freedom to follow my life's Purpose.

I don't believe this was a coincidence. Let's face it. If I had not discovered my Purpose through meditation and was still a complacent person floating through life, and if I were still happy working at my university, you would not be reading these words because they would never have been written. I probably would still think of art as a fun, sometime hobby. I have to contribute this perfect storm of chaos to Divine Timing, just as my dean inviting me to teach at Texas Tech was on that hot July morning in 1998 during my initial Call to Adventure that took me from nonworking wife to independent professor.

I've discovered that once you've realized your Purpose in life and who your True Self is supposed to be, it's really difficult to ignore that little voice inside your heart always urging and pulling you toward your life's Path. Steven Pressfield, author of *The War of Art: Break Through the Blocks and Win Your Inner Creative Battles*, says it's more painful to deny our Purpose once it's known than is the fear of getting to work toward making it happen.

I totally agree. The pain of not following my Purpose was becoming exponentially greater, especially with the extra push of disillusionment I now felt toward my university. I knew I had to do something to alleviate that pain.

My heart began imploring me to not sign the next year's contract at my university. My intuition whispered that if I signed the next contract locking myself into another academic year, it would cause a painful, unnecessary detour just as caving in to having a baby I knew I was not meant to conceive had done. My intuition said that committing to another year at my university would cause a door to slam shut in the face of my life's Purpose.

What in the world was I supposed to do – play small, ignore the Call, and stay at my university? Or take a very scary blind leap of faith into the unknown?

Belly of the Whale

# Belly of the Whale

I made a deal with God on a cold January day in 2015 sitting in my car in the McDonald's drive-through line, waiting for my lunch of two hamburgers and small Diet Coke. I was on my way to teach class at the university at which I'd worked 11 years. I enjoyed my time as a professor there, but I knew in my heart it would be a huge mistake to sign the next contract, which would come out around April and be due with signature in mid-May. If I chose to stay. But I knew I couldn't sign this contract no matter how stupid or illogical or scary it may seem to quit a perfectly stable and prosperous position, and go do what? My intuition was telling me to go become a spiritual life coach, which I've never done before. In fact, I wasn't sure how one even becomes a spiritual life coach or what exactly that job entails.

All I knew was that a week before, I was sitting in the first faculty meeting of the spring semester, totally tuned out to the discussion at hand reading through my personal emails, when BOOM! I saw an email that was like a jolt of electricity piercing my heart. I'd recently watch an Empowered Intuition video offered by Gabrielle Bernstein, spiritual teacher and self-proclaimed Spirit Junkie, which really spoke to me. It said when we're aligned with our Higher Power – in my case God – and allow our intuition to tap into this power, we become a magnet to attract our deepest desires into our lives. This concept wasn't new to me because I've always relied on my intuition, and it had never steered me toward the wrong direction. When I began meditating in March 2013 and eventually discovered that my purpose in life is to use my visual diary art, life experiences, and writing in some way to inspire others to follow their true calling, I wasn't sure exactly how that would happen. But then, during that first faculty meeting of 2015, Gabby's email arrived inviting me to sign up for another free video to learn how to run a spiritual business. "YES!" my heart shouted. This is what I'm meant to do! I can use my teaching skills, art, writing and past life transition from nonworking wife to professor to teach others how to become unstuck in their lives and change their life direction if need be.

And that's how I found myself in the drive-through at McDonald's making a deal with God. I told God that if He would send me a financial solution, hopefully in April around the same time my next contract arrived, that I would happily resign from my university and dedicate the rest of my life to doing what He wanted me to do in this new spiritual teacher capacity and go wherever that would lead. I immediately felt a sense of peace at making this commitment and heard in my mind that it would be done. However, I soon realized that I can't dictate the terms of this deal to God. Duh! I had to totally surrender the fear and outcome my fingertips were so desperately clinging to for this to work.

My intuition assured me that if I took a leap of faith and resigned from my professor position, even with no visible financial safety net in place, the Universe would support me and pave the way toward this new life goal. But my ego - and my mother's voice – crept in with controlling questions and doubt: how will you make money, what about healthcare, what if no one wants to hire you in this new capacity, what if, what if, what if?

Some of you might be asking at this point, "Why couldn't you try weaving your Purpose around your stable job obligations and continue receiving a steady paycheck?" Trust me. I tried for a solid year. I tried making a painting or writing date with myself on Friday nights or Sunday afternoons. I tried tuning out campus obligations until noon on random Tuesday mornings. It still wasn't enough. My teaching and grading commitments, campus committee obligations, plus serving as the chair of my department ended up being a six- to seven-day-a-week time sink. I began to feel more and more frustrated and resentful that my day job was sucking energy away from my dream. I needed to spread my wings to their fullest extent to be able to truly fulfill my Purpose. I know this may not work for some people, but it didn't work for me to try to juggle two existences.

I had to resign to make this work.

In her book, *The Wizard of Us: Transformational Lessons from Oz*, Jean Houston labels this precarious place of predicament as the Belly of the Whale phase of Joseph Campbell's the Hero's Journey. After the heroine on the journey accepts the Call to Adventure, an intuitive summons to make a positive difference in the world, she ventures into an unknown realm, the Belly of the Whale. Here, the heroine may be feeling the urge to make a huge life change, veering into new territory, and exhibits willingness to morph into a better, more enlightened version of herself while dying to the old self.

I recognized my intuition's invitation to evolve, its drumbeat becoming progressively louder and stronger. I had denied that invitation when I didn't follow my intuition and succumbed to becoming pregnant at my mother's insistence even though I knew it was a huge mistake. I followed the drumbeat's call when my intuition said to accept the offer to teach at Texas Tech in 1998 even though I was shaking in my sandals the first day of class. I obeyed my intuition when I cancelled one interview and declined a separate job offer from two universities that I knew were not for me, even before my favored university offered me the professor position I knew was meant to be mine. I bravely followed my intuition when I moved from Texas to Connecticut with no friends or family awaiting me on the Connecticut end of the journey, and my family in Texas thought I was crazy to move so far from home alone. In all of these instances, my intuition had been spot-on correct.

So I knew I couldn't ignore my intuition's summons this time and possibly ruin a chance to experience a wonderful evolution toward my perceived life's Calling, as foggy and uncertain as the road to that Calling was. I began to envision myself as a gardener, whose purpose is to get women unstuck; uproot them from their life circumstances that block them from fulfilling their true life's Purpose. I saw myself pulling them from the ground of their daily ruts and dislodging the roots deeply clinging to their old lives and old perceptions that no longer serve them. I uprooted myself from my previous married circumstance that was slowly smothering me when I walked through an open door and accepted the challenge to become a professor, leaving my old, broken life 1,700 miles in the rearview mirror. However, I knew I wouldn't be able to truly help others become unstuck from their fear-based ruts if I didn't successfully uproot myself again by resigning from my university and pursuing the role I believe I was put on this Earth to accomplish. I knew my credibility would be shot if I were so afraid of the unknown that I remained in the status quo, stuck, unhappy and refusing this more profound Call to Adventure to fulfill my destiny. I would feel completely inauthentic and fake if I tried to advise others to follow their true Purpose when I knew that I was not completely doing that myself. I couldn't rely on the example of a life transition that happened more than a decade ago and expect others to find me a powerful source of inspiration, especially when I knew in my heart that this new evolution would take me closer to fulfilling the reason for why I was born. I had to follow my intuition once again and uproot myself to be able to help others, even if I was unsure of the outcome.

But, the question remained: How do I bridge the gap between my stable, predictable life as a university professor and the goal of using my life experiences, visual diary art, writing, and teaching abilities in this unknown capacity? Two options existed: stay in my professor position with a certain paycheck and suffer because I'm refusing the Call to pursue my destiny, or leap toward freedom. I had to believe that once airborne, I would sprout wings and God would support me, just as He did the last time I took a leap of faith.

On February 24, 2015, I resigned from my very secure 11-year, tenured professor position to dive into the unknown abyss of following this second, more profound Call to Adventure. Had I figured out all of the details of exactly how this would play out and work? Nope. All I knew in every fiber of my being was that if I didn't make this shift toward my True Self, my soul would shrivel within me and die.

I was officially and deeply ensconced in the Belly of the Whale.

No Regrets

# A Long and Winding Dot-filled Road

Many things have happened since February 24, 2015, when I resigned from my university position. I've come to truly appreciate Steve Jobs' quote, "You can't connect the dots looking forward; you can only connect them looking backwards. So you have to trust that the dots will somehow connect in your future."

Since resigning, I've collected a lot of dots.

Gabrielle Bernstein's Spirit Junkie teachings led me to Marie Forleo's B-School, an online course that instructs heart-centered entrepreneurs how to conduct online marketing. But what was my heart-centered business going to be exactly? When people asked me what I was going to do after resigning, I began trying on the coat of saying I would become a life coach. Since discovering what a life coach was via Gabby Bernstein, I had hired one of my own who prompted me to have the courage to kiss my university contract goodbye and move toward my desired destiny. I truly understood from first-hand experience how a life coach can help a person move toward life goals through well-placed action steps. A very valuable service! So, I decided to become one. I enrolled in a 12-week, intensive life coach training that started the same week that final exams took place during the last spring semester I was employed at my university. Perfect timing!

But where was my art in this new life coaching plan? I formulated the idea that I could develop and offer Honor Your Purpose art workshops, designed to help women identify and cultivate their True Self and Purpose through art journaling and a juicy Vision Canvas painting, a symbol to remind them to honor their Purpose. I had many year's experience creating class schedules and new course offerings as a professor, so developing and teaching art workshops seemed a logical next step.

But, had I ever done art journaling myself? Nope. So, I enrolled in several online art journaling classes to see what it was all about. I discovered that art journaling, similar to my past canvas painting experiences, can be a purging, emotional release. Art journaling is a for-your-eyes-only vehicle that can help one express feelings and perceptions in a way that talking or writing about them cannot. The art combined with life coaching would be a powerful pairing to allow women in my art workshops to alchemize their gifts and obstacles into something that would heal their soul and move them toward fulfilling their life's Calling. So, I began developing a workshop curriculum that I planned to offer in art studios in the US and abroad.

My plan seemed rock-solid. All the dots were seamlessly lining up into perfect order! When the 12-week life coach training ended in mid-August, I began creating promotional materials for my art workshops that I feverishly emailed to several art organizations and studios. My last university paycheck would arrive on August 31st, and I was certain that I would make a smooth transition into booking and teaching my art workshops, while attracting ideal life coaching clients. During the summer, I had learned about visualizing my dreams and placing myself in the feeling - the vibration - of how it would be to see those dreams manifest into reality. I thought, this time I have worked hand-in-hand with my intuition to easily morph into my True Self and live my life's Purpose!

But then…nothing happened.

One nonprofit arts organization near Seattle agreed to host my Honor Your Purpose art workshop, but it was eventually cancelled due to low enrollment. Other arts organizations expressed that my workshops sounded like a great opportunity, but none followed through on my pleas to actually book the workshop.

No one hired me as a life coach, although I had promoted my Heroine's Journey story and life coaching packages on several social media outlets. My story, always accompanied by one of my paintings, was met with positive response on social media, and a couple of women expressed interest in free discovery calls to discuss how life coaching could benefit their lives. But one was a no show on the discovery call and the other declined my offer. No one else expressed interest.

I knew it's the norm for new businesses to start slow and experience hiccups along the way, but something else was going on. My intuition perceived a formidable brick wall in every direction. I began to perceive that no promotion I tried would end in booking clients or workshops. Something was totally off. Was I moving in the wrong direction?

I found myself increasingly lost, confused and left wondering if I had bought a bag of defunct magical beans. What had I done? My secure professor position was left miles behind in the dust. I had no income coming in, a prospect that left me frozen in fear of what to do next.

Once again, I found myself on the bathroom floor imploring God for guidance.

The message my heart perceived was to be still, surrender and listen. Connect the dots.

Je Suis un Artiste

# Je Suis un Artiste

Two weeks passed. I cried, fretted, felt weak and deeply confused. I had the nagging feeling that there was something I wasn't seeing, something larger looming beyond my limited field of perception. Was my intuition faulty? This scared me to death, because I had always relied so heavily on its guidance. Had I misread the signs this time and made a huge mistake? What if I had collected the wrong dots!

But then clarity finally began to slowly rise over the foggy horizon as I succumbed to getting still, surrendering and listening. I remembered one of my good friends had given me a magazine article about a local art gallery inviting artists to submit portfolios of their artwork. After reading the article, which had been sitting forgotten on my kitchen counter, my life's Purpose flooded into my mind.

What was the clear-as-a-bell answer that entered my consciousness during Deepak's meditation in summer 2013 asking if no fear or obstacles existed, what would I be? What did my 6-year-old self answer during the Little Miss Happy beauty contest when the judge asked what I wanted to be when I grew up?

Both answers were exactly the same – "an artist."

I slowly began to realize that once again, I had pushed my art to the back burner as a part-time hobby. I was an artist who was not creating any art.

I thought back to the conversations I'd had during the summer. I remembered that when I described the mission of my art workshops to people – a mission I truly believe in - I was quick to say that the workshops were not meant to teach my art technique, but to use art as a tool to inspire women to discover their life's path. Of course I would use some of my visual diary portraits to illustrate my story of evolution as an introduction to the workshops, but my art was definitely not the focus. I had not been willing to admit it to myself, but my heart knew down deep in that moment of clarity that my quickness to downplay my own art stemmed from a long-standing limiting belief that people would perceive my memoir portraits as not good enough for public display.

I was creating art workshops to use art as a tool to teach others to find their life Purpose, but I was denying my Purpose by not creating art myself. I was making the unilateral move of morphing from a professor teaching in a university classroom to a life coach teaching in an art workshop setting, while having the cool part-time hobby of art.

This trajectory was not honoring my own life Purpose of BEING an artist. I realized that I had a major block toward becoming a true artist who could exhibit and sell her work. The limiting beliefs that I had heard throughout life came tumbling forward, and I was buying into the beliefs that claimed my work is not good enough to publically show or sell. No one would want to purchase my art to hang on the walls of their own home. Art was a frivolous hobby that should be left till retirement.

I had to change the belief about who my True Self was.

I also realized that my intuition wasn't faulty, and I had not bought a bag of defunct magical beans. I had simply visualized a dream that was too small, too restricting. My underlying fear that chugged in my mind like a train when my university paycheck dried up - I gotta make money, I gotta make money, I gotta make money – had caused me to accept the unilateral move of professor to art workshop teacher, a move that may be familiar and easily doable, but one that would not allow me to grow. The Universe was urging me to expand way beyond my perceived limits and accept a dream that I believed was unreal, impossible, and out of reach.

I also perceived that I had been waiting for a grand gesture from the Universe to swoop in and save my financial day. In 1998, when I was at rock bottom as a nonworking wife in a failing marriage who had just lost a baby I was not meant to conceive, the dean at Texas Tech University had swooped in and changed my life forever by asking me to teach a summer writing course and by suggesting I earn a doctorate degree.

However, no grand gesture was coming this time. The Universe was sending me little breadcrumb clues – subtle whispers, mini-steps toward my Destiny – that I was meant to pay attention to and follow. The Universe was quietly giving me the numbers and order that would eventually unlock my Destiny's combination lock, although the entire combination would not be given all at once. In this second, more profound Call to Adventure, the Universe was telling me that I'd matured in awareness and intuition, so the solution would not simply fall into my lap. It was up to me to get still, surrender and listen.

When I got still, surrendered and listened, I began to perceive that I had collected a basket full of breadcrumb clues – the magazine article about the art gallery that reminded me of my artist Purpose, an email from my mentor-friend inviting me to attend the Connecticut meeting of the National Speaker Association, the book contract I had signed with Balboa Press during the summer that I had put aside thinking I'd start this book during the holidays.

And suddenly, a light bulb came on in my mind and my path became much clearer. I want to be a true artist who routinely and passionately creates new art and exhibits and sells her work. So, I began researching art galleries and meeting people who could educate me about this new world.

I want to write this book that will tell the story of my Heroine's Journey and illustrate key moments with my memoir art. So, I started scheduling writing time into my weekly calendar and began writing immediately instead of waiting until a future chunk of time magically appeared during the holidays.

Learning about the National Speaker Association meetings created a bolt of excitement in my heart, and I realized I want to become a public speaker to spread the message that it is possible to live your life's Purpose and dream. So, I began attending monthly meetings to learn about the speaking field and tools to book engagements.

And, of course, I want to teach my Honor Your Purpose art workshops in the US and abroad and use art combined with life coaching to help women identify and cultivate their gifts that they were given at birth to make the world a better place.

What I've learned from this process – and it is a process that requires awareness, navigation, and thought, not a quick fix – is that I must surrender to the fact that God can dream a much larger dream for me than my limited, human vision will allow. The devastation and fear that I felt when my art workshop plan didn't immediately pan out was really a Divine Gift that asked me to expand beyond my perceived boundaries and small thinking. It was time for me to greatly beef up my faith and trust in God's plan for my life to fulfill the Purpose for why He created me.

This beautiful realization came a few days before my 50th birthday on October 20th, 2015. At midnight, just as my birthday was dawning, I made a new deal with God. I'm so very grateful that He gave me the courage to resign from my very secure professor position to venture down this road toward my True Self and life's Purpose. And even though I still can't see the outcome and on some days I'm still shaking in my boots from fear and what-ifs, I surrender to the process of figuring it out. I surrender to the message my intuition whispers to me that urges me to remain on this path, write this book, create my art, continue looking for the next right step, even it seems counterproductive to not seek another predictable job with a secure paycheck.

I believe there's a time to sow and a time to reap. Now is my time to sow creativity and prepare for the coming harvest of my creative efforts.

All I have to do is remain on the path and listen with an open heart.

Black Sheep Evolution

# Gotta Pay It Forward

Did you know that we ALL have a Purpose in life?

Yep, that means you too.

Joseph Campbell said it best: "Follow your bliss and the Universe will open doors where there were only walls." What is your bliss – that unique gift, your Purpose - that the Universe gave you at birth that you are meant to use to serve the world and make it a better place?

You're not meant to keep your fabulous gift to yourself hidden like a candle under a bushel. You're supposed to let your Purpose shine and illuminate the world! The final step of the Hero's Journey is that you return from your adventure to teach others what you've learned.

So, here are a few of the lessons I've learned - so far - while traveling the road of following my bliss of art that can hopefully help you as you navigate your own Heroine's (or Hero's) Journey.

*Glenda the Good Witch was right. You do have the power within you!*

If you're uncertain what your unique gift is, look to your childhood. What did you love to do that made your heart sing and time fly? Even if you haven't done that activity in years, the desire is still within you. Pull it out of your soul's closet, dust it off, and give it a whirl! Those activities that give you pure joy are breadcrumb clues to your life's Purpose.

*Don't let the naysayers rain on your parade.*

We all have that Inner Critic and people in our lives who say, "You'll never be able to pull that off. Are you crazy?" Don't listen! Whether it's your Inner Critic, mom, spouse, or grumpy next-door neighbor, there will be people in your life who just won't understand your urge to live your Purpose. These people want you to remain small and not change so they won't have to acknowledge their own soul's calling. Surround yourself with people who recognize your gift and encourage you to spread your wings and fly!

*Meditation can help you tap into your intuition.*

As I've described, meditation has been a life changer for me. In that auspicious meditation session during summer 2013 when Deepak asked if I could be anything in life, what would that be, my path toward manifesting my Destiny of being an artist began. Meditation will help you perceive your soul's voice, lead you to your Calling, and gradually illuminate the steps to make it happen.

*Expect miracles to occur when you say YES! to living your Purpose.*

Joseph Campbell said that he perceived "invisible hands" that began opening new doors when he agreed to follow his bliss. I've found this to be true. At just the perfect moment when I need guidance, a book, person, light bulb moment, or opportunity crosses my path. The Universe will conspire to help you when you commit to following your Purpose too.

*Sorry, the S word is absolutely necessary when discovering and living your Purpose.*

I've always been told: "Ask, believe, receive." The problem is, sometimes what I ask for may not be in my best interest – aligned with a Greater Plan for my life. So, no matter how much I believe it could or needs to happen, sometimes what I ask for and believe in receives the answer of no. This can be disheartening, but if I stop the pity party and think, I realize I don't have the power to see into the future. Thank goodness the Universe has got my back even when I feel disappointed! It may be guiding me toward a better path, helping me avoid a disaster I couldn't perceive, or teaching me a lesson I needed to learn before advancing to the next step of the Greater Plan.

So, I'd like to add in one element: "Ask, believe, *surrender*, receive." Surrendering is really difficult for me, because patience is not one of my virtues. But, since I've placed myself in the exhilarating and sometimes terrifying position of becoming an entrepreneur and living my Purpose, I have no choice but to fully surrender to a Greater Plan that I can't see. Life is like shaking a Polaroid photo – I only get one glimpse of the next right step at a time. The fuller map is blurry and masked. I'm learning that living with uncertainty is inevitable and OK.

I believe that miracles happen every day. But sometimes when I'm in the fear zone of not being able to see the future, but really wanting to control it, I lose sight of the tiny miracles that pop up leading to larger ones. Fear can cause me to think, "Who am I to receive something wonderful? That could never happen to me."

Then I remember this beautiful quote by Marianne Williamson, author of *A Return to Love*:

"Our deepest fear is not that we are inadequate. Our deepest fear is that we are powerful beyond measure. It is our light, not our darkness that most frightens us. We ask ourselves, Who am I to be brilliant, gorgeous, talented, fabulous? Actually, who are you not to be? You are a child of God. Your playing small does not serve the world. There is nothing enlightened about shrinking so that other people won't feel insecure around you. We are all meant to shine, as children do. We were born to make manifest the glory of God within us. It's not just in some of us; it's in everyone. And as we let our own light shine, we unconsciously give other people permission to do the same. As we are liberated from our own fear, our presence automatically liberates others."

It's not just about us my friends. It's about the – dare I say it? – the miracles that can occur through us if we surrender and allow them to flow. That's what living your Purpose is all about.

Genora Genius – in honor of Vicki's Grandmother

# Honor Your Purpose Action Steps

Write your answers to the questions below, or visit http://vickiworldart.com/honor-your-purpose-action-sheet/ for a downloadable Honor Your Purpose Action Sheet PDF. You'll also find a downloadable version of my Freedom mini-portrait, my gift to you! While you're on my website, sign up for my email list to receive updates about my art, Honor Your Purpose art workshops, and speaking engagements!

If no fear or limitations existed, what would you most like to do with your life? In other words, what is the unique gift – the Purpose - that you would love to share with the world?

_____

_____

_____

List at least 3 obstacles that hinder you from fulfilling your Purpose.

_____

_____

_____

_____

What are mini-steps you can take each day, week, month to help you work toward fulfilling your Purpose? (i.e. - attend workshops, schedule YOU time in calendar, start a Facebook group of like-minded people, etc.)

_____

_____

_____

_____

Identify the values that are important to you to live a balanced, happy life. (My top 3 are freedom to work on projects that are important to me, creativity, meaningful contribution.) Do your values match your Purpose and the mini-steps you listed to achieve that Purpose? If not, how can you tweak your action plan to make all areas work together?

_____

_____

_____

_____

4" x 6" Freedom mini-portrait

# Honor Your Purpose Art Project

Cut a piece of paper or poster board into a 4" x 6" rectangle. (This is a common size for cute, embellished photo frames.)

Draw symbols that have special meaning to you – flowers, birds, butterflies, numbers, inspirational words or quotes, etc. - with markers or craft paint in colors you love and/or glue magazine photos of your special symbols on your rectangle. Your symbols should represent your True Self and Purpose emerging.

Frame your creation and place it in a room you frequent daily – your office, bedroom, bathroom – as a reminder to honor and cultivate your True Self and life's Purpose.

Resistance Warrior/Muse Morph

# About the Author

Vicki Todd is a memoir artist, Ed.D., and life coach. She teaches Honor Your Purpose art workshops designed to help women identify and cultivate their True Self and life Purpose through art journaling exercises and a Vision Canvas painting, a reminder to live their Purpose. In addition to authoring *Unstuck: One Heroine's Journey of Art and the Courage to Live on Purpose*, Vicki wrote a chapter in *20 Beautiful Women Volume 2: 20 More Stories that Will Heal Your Soul, Ignite Your Passion, and Inspire Your Divine Purpose*. She has also been a featured blogger in the Huffington Post. In addition, Vicki is a motivational speaker.

You can view Vicki's visual diary portraits on her website, http://vickiworldart.com/

If you would like to purchase Vicki's artwork or request a commissioned portrait, please contact Vicki at vickiworldart@gmail.com.

If you would like to book Vicki as a motivational speaker, please email her at vickiworldart@gmail.com.

If you wish to schedule Vicki's Honor Your Purpose art workshop, offered in group and one-on-one VIP settings, please email her at vickiworldart@gmail.com.

You can connect with Vicki on Facebook, Instagram and Twitter @vickiworldart.

Printed in the United States
By Bookmasters